Real World Blackjack

Real World Blackjack

How to Win at Blackjack
Without Counting Cards

John Lucas

To order additional copies of this book, contact:
Xlibris Corporation
1-888-795-4274
www.Xlibris.com
Orders@Xlibris.com
109907

CONTENTS

CHAPTER 1

Overview

I HAVE BEEN a Blackjack Dealer for approximately twenty years. According to my calculations, over this period of time, I have dealt out over six million hands of Blackjack to tens of thousands of customers. I have seen hundreds, if not thousands, of different betting and playing strategies. I have seen players that never seem to win, while others that seem to win more consistently. The purpose in writing this book is to assist players to play smarter, bet more wisely, and to win more often. From my twenty years of observation, and my own meticulous research that spanned several years, I believe that over the long run people can win at Blackjack without counting cards. If you read this book and follow it's advice, you too can be a winning Blackjack player. Even though there are no guarantees, my research and the program I have developed, has consistently worked for me, and I believe it can work for you.

Twenty years ago, when I was first trained to become a Blackjack Dealer, I immediately found the game fascinating, as have thousands of other gamblers. I read a number of quality books at that time that included : Beat the Dealer by Edwin Thorpe, Million Dollar Blackjack by Ken Uston, Playing Blackjack As a Business by Lawrence Revere, and The World's Greatest Blackjack Book by Lance Humble. Since then I have continued to read many of the newly published Blackjack books. Some of these are excellent, with great information, others I consider somewhat weak when it comes to providing any useful new ideas. One of the more recent books I have read and enjoyed immensely was, The Big Book of Blackjack by Arnold Snyder.

One of the first thing I did twenty years ago was to memorize the most common Basic Strategy chart that informs a player on how to play each hand of Blackjack that they may receive. A good Basic Strategy will give the player the best odds as whether to hit, stay, double, or split on any hand they encounter. The player will look at their two card total and also the dealer's up card to determine the best course of action. As in all gambling, it all comes down to odds. By playing the best odds, a player will greatly increase their chances of winning over the long run. Since playing a consistent Basic Strategy will give the player the best chance of winning, I found it and still do find it interesting in watching how players play in relation to the most common Basic Strategy. Even though there are a few variations on Basic Strategy depending on the number of decks being used, when you can double, how many times you can split Aces, is surrender available, and a few more variables, I have never seen a player follow the most common Basic Strategy that can be found in the previously mentioned books 100% of the time. Even a good Basic Strategy player always seems to have one or two situations where they go their own way and don't follow Basic Strategy. I have also noticed that the players that consistently win more and conversely lose less are those that play a consistent Basic Strategy "hand in and hand out".

Why do I call this book "Real World Blackjack"? That is because the research I conducted, that will be detailed in the coming pages, uses Real World conditions. What are Real World conditions? Real World conditions include the following:

1. The number of players at the table. Sometimes you may play for a long period of time just one on one with the dealer. Most of the time you will be playing with others that might include a full table of seven players. When playing with others, you may have players occasionally sitting out a few hands, or maybe even adding hands by playing multiple spots. You may have others popping in and out for a few hands and leaving the table. This constant fluctuation of players during a shoe or a playing session is almost unavoidable, but this is the reality in the Real World of playing Blackjack.

2. How do other players play their hands? Besides the fluctuation of the number of players you may play with, there is also the variation of how these players play their hands. Are most of these players playing a good Basic Strategy or are there some loose cannons that are playing by intuition or simply have no clue at all. Again, these are Real World conditions. Whenever you play Blackjack, the other players at the table will have their own ways of playing, sometimes following a Basic Strategy a good portion of the time, but more likely there will be a few that will be playing less than a consistent Basic Strategy.

All of the research, calculations, and advice in this book have been determined by considering these varying "Real World" conditions. The areas I will be detailing that will give the readers of this book the foundation on how to win consistently at Blackjack are; Basic Strategy, Betting Strategies, and Money Management. Let me say a few words about each of these areas before I go into detail.

Basic Strategy: Does the Basic Strategy that is printed in many Blackjack books hold up under the fluctuating Real World conditions that I have previously explained? I dealt out 10,000 hands using these fluctuating Real World conditions to determine whether a player should hit, stay, double, or split in every situation. For example, should a player hit or stand with a total of "16" versus a dealer's "10" up card? I dealt out 10,000 hands that kept track of the wins, pushes, and loses when a player would stay with a "16" vs "10", and also when a player would hit with a "16"vs"10". The players "16" was sometimes a two card "16" as a "9-7" or a "10-6", other times it was a three, four, or five card "16". I also varied the number of players at the table and varied how the other players played their hands to replicate Real World conditions. If a player bet "one unit" for each of these 10,000 hands, I could, by looking at the final results, determine whether the player should hit or stay in this Real World situation.

In dealing 10,000 hands for each hand possibility (yes, this took me a long long time), I determined my Real World Basic Strategy. This strategy will show the player how to optimally play each hand that is dealt to them. How does my Real World Basic Strategy compare to the more common Basic Strategies that are found in books and on the internet? This analysis will be detailed in the Basic Strategy chapter.

Betting Strategies: After learning how to play each hand using Real World Basic Strategy, then how much should you bet each hand. I have seen numerous betting strategies over my twenty years of dealing, from players who mostly bet the same flat bet hand in and hand out, to others who will increase their bet conservatively during a winning streak, to those are very aggressive in increasing their bet, and even those who like to only increase their bet after they have lost three, four, or more hands in a row. Besides my many years of observing many betting strategies, I also dealt out over 200,000 hands and kept track of the wins and loses. I plugged these wins and loses into twenty of the most common betting strategies

I have observed and determined whether there was one betting strategy that would consistently give the player a winning edge. The results will be detailed in the Betting Strategy chapter of this book.

Money Management: Money Management is just as important in being a consistent winner at Blackjack as playing the correct Basic Strategy and using an optimal Betting Strategy. Money Management consists of two areas. One is determining how much a player should buy in for and setting winning limits and conversely losing limits. Secondly, is it advantageous to set a time limit, and quit after this time limit is met, whether the player is a head or behind? My recommendations will be detailed in the Money Management chapter of this book. These recommendations will be based on my my years of observation of players who seem to consistently win more and lose less, and also of my 200,000 hand analysis that kept track of the win/loss scenarios using my Real World Basic Strategy and my Real World Betting Strategy.

These three areas; Basic Strategy, Betting Strategy, and Money Management will be explained in their respective chapters. To play winning Blackjack, all three have equal importance. Just to concentrate on one or two areas but ignoring the other area will not result in you winning consistently.

If you would play an excellent Basic Strategy but ignore the Betting Strategy or Money Management area, your results will be less than adequate. Learn and apply all three areas to your play, and I feel you will make money playing Blackjack. This will take patience, discipline, and commitment, but I believe you will reap the rewards of your effort. Though the results are not guaranteed, I believe that if you follow my advice, keep records, you will see that you are consistently playing winning Blackjack. It has worked for me, and my motivation for writing this book is that it will for others who enjoy playing Blackjack and enjoy winning in the long run.

CHAPTER 2

Real World Basic Strategy

WE ARE NOW going to explore on how a player should play each Blackjack hand they encounter. How each hand is played is determined by the player looking at their initial two card total and then looking at the dealer's up card, and then determining whether they should hit, stay, double down, or split. The decision that gives the player the best odds in every situation is called Basic Strategy. I am going to assume that the readers of this book know the basic rules of Blackjack. I assume you know what it means to hit, stay, double down, split, what a soft hand is, etc. I have dealt to thousands of people, and the overwhelming majority know the basic rules and concepts of Blackjack.

If you are going to be a successful Blackjack player, you must play by making decisions using the most favorable odds as a basis for your playing decisions. I have witnessed this time and time again. The best Blackjack players that win the most, play a consistent Basic Strategy hand in and hand out. Those that play by intuition, guessing, or some other theory are consistent losers. The sad part is that these players seem to have no clue as to why they always seem to lose. Even when these players are given good advice by other players and even the dealer, they remain stubborn in their way of doing things and consistently lose time and time again. If you recognize yourself as this type of player, may I suggest you try the methods and advice you will find in this book and see what happens. What have you got to lose, since what you have been doing time and again doesn't seem to be working.

The Basic Strategy I have developed is based on what I have found to be the most prevalent Blackjack rules in the Casinos I have worked and played. These rules are: the use of a six deck shoe, players can double down on any two cards, players can split any two cards of equal value up to four hands, players can double after a split, dealer hits a soft 17, and Blackjack pays 3 to 2.

The Basic Strategy that you will read in many books are based on computer analysis. Each hand situation has been run through a computer to determine whether a player should hit, stay, double, or split. My Real World Basic Strategy was determined by dealing 10,000 hands for each Blackjack hand situation and determining whether a player should hit, stay, double, or split using Real World conditions. As explained earlier, Real World conditions include a number of uncontrollable variables as:

1) how many players at the table and how are they playing.
2) are they playing a solid Basic Strategy or are some of them playing by intuition or some other inconsistent theory.
3) are players coming in the middle of the shoe for just a few hands.
4) are the players at the table constantly changing the number of spots they are playing by sometimes playing two or three spots or sometimes sitting out a hand or two.

As a Blackjack player, you may prefer to only play by yourself or just with one or two other players all the time, but as any player knows this is not going to happen in the Real World Casino environment. You are going to be playing with all the changing variables that I have just described.

My Real World Basic Strategy will vary in only a few instances from the computer based Basic Strategy. I will print out both Basic Strategy charts in the coming pages and will explain these few situations where my research advises you to play certain hands differently from the computer model.

I computed how to play each hand situation by dealing out 10,000 hands, betting one unit per hand, using the varying Real World conditions previously described. I then calculated the win/loss outcome if a player hit, stayed, doubled, or split for each hand situation. After playing 10,000 hands, betting 10,000 units, it was easy to determine what playing decision you should follow. For instance, if you would have more betting units remaining by hitting as opposed to staying in a specific situation, then you should obviously always hit when this situation occurs.

This is how I will present the results of my research. Even though I dealt out 10,000 hands betting one unit per hand for each Blackjack hand situation, I averaged the results to reflect what would happen every 1,000 hands. I found the results were easier to see using this 1,000 hand average. Consider the following chart.

16 VS. 10

	STAY	HIT
W	209	205
P	-	44
L	791	751
UR	418	454

Let me explain this chart in detail. This chart reflects on what would happen if a player had a total of "16" versus a dealer's "10" up card. It shows the results of what would happen if you hit or stayed. This is an average of doing this for 1,000 hands betting one unit each hand. The "W" stands for the player winning the hand, "P" stands for the hand pushing, "L" stands for losing the hand, and "UR" stands for Units Remaining.

If a player played 1,000 hands, betting one unit per hand, and "Stayed" on a "16" vs. "10", the player would win 209 hands/units, would lose 791 hands/units, with the player ending up with 418 Units Remaining from the original 1,000 units that the player started with.

This is the formula:
Original Units   1,000
Add Wins . . . . . .   +   209
Minus Loses . . . . . .   -   791
Units Remaining   418

If the player would Hit a "16" vs. "10", again averaging out betting one unit for 1,000 hands, the player would win 205 hands/units, push 44 hands/units, and lose 751 hands/units. The player would end up after 1,000 hands with 454 units.

The formula:

Original Units		1,000
Add Wins	+	205
Minus losses	-	751
Units Remaining		454

You can see that out of the original 1,000 units, you would end up with 454 units if you hit a "16" vs. "10", or 418 units if you stay with a "16" vs. "10". Therefore, you should always hit a "16" vs. "10". You gain 36 units every 1,000 times you do this, or to reduce it further, you will gain 3.6 units every 100 times this situation occurs. If you play Blackjack a lot, you will face this particular situation easily 1,000 times over the months you play. If you were a $10 player, you would end up with $360 more in your pocket after 1,000 hands by hitting versus staying. If you were a $25 player, you would gain $900, and if you were a $100 player, you would gain $3,600 by hitting in this situation. Always hit a "16" vs. "10".

One interesting fact by looking at this chart more closely, is that you will actually outright win less hitting "16" vs "10" (209 wins by staying to 205 by hitting). The reason you end up with more Units Remaining when you hit is that you will push 44 hands when you hit. These push units are betting units that remain in your bank.

Let's look at another "16" vs. "10" situation. What if your "16" total is the result of a pair of "8's". Should you hit or split in this situation? You have heard that you should always split a pair of "8's" in every situation. Let's see how this works in the Real World. When you split "8's", you may get another "8" and could split again up to four hands. You may also double down on these splits if the right opportunity arises. Here are the results of splitting a pair of "8's" versus a "10".

16 VS. 10

	STAY	HIT	SPLIT "8's"
W	209	205	618
P	-	44	178
L	791	751	1030
UR	418	454	588

By splitting "8's" in this situation, you would end up with 588 units after 1,000 hands, as opposed to 454 Units Remaining if you hit. You will gain 134 units by splitting "8's" vs. "10" every 1,000 times this occurs as opposed to hitting. So you should always split a pair of "8's" vs. a "10", while always hitting any other "16" vs. "10".If you were a $10 player you would gain $1,340 by splitting versus hitting every one thousand times this occurs.

Now let's look at one more possibility to consider when faced with a "16" vs. "10". If the Casino offers "surrender", should you take it. Surrender is when you take no action on your hand. By surrendering, you lose one half your bet and your hand is over. If you surrendered each time you had a "16" vs. "10", you would end up with 500 Units Remaining after 1,000 hands. Compare this to the 454 Units Remaining you would have if you hit. In this case you would gain 46 units per 1,000 hands by surrendering. So you should always surrender (if allowed) a "16" vs. "10", unless you have a pair of "8's" in which case you should split.

Let us look at a few more situations that are many times misplayed. The first one to consider is when a player has a "soft 17" versus a dealer's "7". Even many good players tend to stay in this situation, just hoping for a push. Here are the calculations.

SOFT 17 VS. 7

	STAY	HIT
W	278	431
P	352	165
L	370	404
UR	908	1027

As you can see, you should always hit a soft "17" vs. "7". You will gain 119 units per 1,000 hands when this occurs.

What about a "12" vs "2" situation? It seems about half the players will hit this, while the other half will stay. Here are the results.

12 VS. 2

	STAY	HIT	SPLIT "6's"
W	347	354	953
P	-	48	49
L	653	598	1157
UR	694	756	796

If you have a "12" that is not composed by a pair of "6's", you should always hit. You will gain 62 units per 1,000 hands by hitting. If your "12" is made up by a pair of "6's", you should split the "6's". You will gain 40 units over hitting in this situation and 102 units over staying. Again, when splitting any pair, you have the possibility of splitting up to four hands and doubling after your splits.

Another situation that I often see misplayed is when the player has an "11" total versus an dealer's "Ace" up card. Many players believe you should always double an "11" against any dealer's up card. In fact, I have seen some Basic Strategies that say this is the correct move. Here are my Real World calculations.

11 VS. ACE

	HIT	DOUBLE
W	490	952
P	111	67
L	399	914
UR	1091	1038

When faced with this hand, just hit and don't double. You will gain 53 units per 1,000 times this situation occurs.

Another misplayed hand is when the player has a soft "18" versus a dealer's "10". Most people stay in this situation, believing that an "18" is a good hand. Here are the calculations.

SOFT 18 VS. 10

	STAY	HIT
W	337	346
P	111	111
L	552	543
UR	785	803

You will gain 18 units per 1,00 hands by hitting a soft "18" vs. "10". As you will see when looking at all of my calculations on the coming pages, you should also hit a soft "18" vs. a "9" and an "Ace".

What if you have a pair of "9's" for a total of "18" vs. a dealers "9". Common sense seems to point to staying with this hand. Here are the results.

PAIR "9's" VS. 9

	STAY	SPLIT "9's"
W	382	662
P	100	242
L	518	722
UR	864	940

You will gain 76 units per 1,000 hands by splitting a pair of "9's" vs. a dealer's "9". Over 1,000 hands, this would be a gain over staying of $380 for a $5 player, $1900 for a $25 player, and $7,600 for a $100 player. Making the correct decision time and again will significantly effect your bankroll for the positive.

Lastly, let's look at a player who has two "10" value cards for a total of "20" vs. a dealer's "6". As most players know, this is a great situation for the player, and they should stay. What players also know is that they will run into other players who want to split their pair of "10's" vs. a "6". Let's see the outcome of this move.

SPLIT "10's" VS. 6

	STAY	SPLIT "10's"
W	806	1006
P	110	97
L	84	480
UR	1722	1526

What is interesting is that whether you stay with a pair of "10's" or split them, you will make a positive gain per 1,000 hands. If you split, you will gain 526 units per 1,000 hands, while by staying you will gain 722 units. So overall, by staying instead of splitting, you will gain 196 units. Obviously, never split a pair of "10's".

On the following pages are many of the results from my research. It is from these results that I determined my Real World Basic Strategy. Again, I dealt out 10,000 hands for each situation using the varying Real World conditions that I described earlier. These charts are averaged down to reflect what would happen every 1,000 times this hand occurred.

One other variable I used when dealing out these hands was to vary the number of cards it took to get a certain hand total. For example, when looking at analyzing a "16" vs. "10", I varied how many cards it took to add up to "16". Sometimes I used a two card "16" as a "9" and "7" or a "10" and "6". Other times I use three, four, or more cards to reach a total of "16". This again reflects Real World conditions.

16 VS. 7

	STAY	HIT
W	276	277
P	-	58
L	724	665
UR	552	612

HIT 16 VS. 7

16 VS. 8

	STAY	HIT
W	249	238
P	-	47
L	751	715
UR	498	523

HIT 16 VS. 8

16 VS. 9

	STAY	HIT	SPLIT 8's
W	212	202	582
P	-	69	174
L	788	729	1040
UR	424	473	542

HIT 16 VS. 9
SPLIT 8's VS. 9

16 VS. 10

	STAY	HIT	SPLIT 8's
W	209	205	618
P	-	44	178
L	791	751	1030
UR	418	454	588

HIT 16 VS. 10
SPLIT 8's VS. 10

16 VS. ACE

	STAY	HIT	SPLIT 8's
W	198	186	494
P	-	52	216
L	802	762	944
UR	396	424	550

HIT 16 VS. ACE
SPLIT 8's VS. ACE

SOFT 18 VS. 9

	STAY	HIT
W	357	391
P	121	107
L	522	502
UR	835	889

HIT SOFT 18 VS. 9

SOFT 18 VS. 10

	STAY	HIT
W	337	346
P	111	111
L	552	543
UR	785	803

HIT SOFT 18 VS. 10

SOFT 18 VS. ACE

	STAY	HIT
W	321	370
P	188	105
L	491	525
UR	830	845

HIT SOFT 18 VS. ACE

12 VS. 2

	STAY	HIT	SPLIT 6's
W	347	354	953
P	-	48	49
L	653	598	1157
UR	694	756	796

HIT 12 VS. 2
SPLIT 6's VS. 2

12 VS. 3

	STAY	HIT
W	383	379
P	-	43
L	617	578
UR	766	801

HIT 12 VS. 3

10 VS. 9

	HIT	DOUBLE
W	508	948
P	100	80
L	392	892
UR	1116	1056

HIT 10 VS. 9

11 VS. 10

	HIT	DOUBLE
W	498	1072
P	90	61
L	412	806
UR	1086	1266

DOUBLE 11 VS. 10

11 VS. ACE

	HIT	DOUBLE
W	490	952
P	111	67
L	399	914
UR	1091	1038

HIT 11 VS. ACE

PAIR "9's" VS 7

	STAY	SPLIT
W	632	916
P	130	247
L	238	561
UR	1394	1355

STAY WITH PAIR
9's VS. 7

PAIR "9's" VS 8

	STAY	SPLIT
W	348	742
P	383	285
L	269	613
UR	1079	1129

SPLIT 9's VS. 8

PAIR "9's" VS 9

	STAY	SPLIT
W	382	662
P	100	242
L	518	722
UR	864	940

SPLIT 9's VS. 9

9 VS. 7

	HIT	**DOUBLE**
W	575	970
P	130	70
L	295	890
UR	1280	1080

HIT 9 VS. 7

10 VS. 8

	HIT	**DOUBLE**
W	520	1048
P	88	64
L	392	824
UR	1128	1224

DOUBLE 10 VS. 8

10 VS. ACE

	HIT	**DOUBLE**
W	464	854
P	181	118
L	355	910
UR	1109	944

HIT 10 VS. ACE

SOFT 17 VS. 2

	HIT	**DOUBLE**
W	467	902
P	77	83
L	456	932
UR	1011	970

HIT SOFT 17 VS. 2

SOFT 17 VS. 3

	HIT	DOUBLE
W	446	952
P	88	72
L	466	904
UR	980	1048

DOUBLE SOFT 17 VS. 3

SOFT 17 VS. 7

	STAY	HIT
W	278	431
P	352	165
L	370	404
UR	908	1027

HIT SOFT 17 VS. 7

SOFT 16 VS. 3

	HIT	DOUBLE
W	478	1011
P	48	39
L	474	911
UR	1004	1100

DOUBLE SOFT 16 VS. 3

SOFT 18 VS. 2

	STAY	DOUBLE
W	506	928
P	134	68
L	360	936
UR	1146	992

STAY SOFT 18 VS. 2

SOFT 18 VS. 3

	STAY	**DOUBLE**
W	544	1096
P	116	68
L	340	768
UR	1204	1328

DOUBLE SOFT 18 VS. 3

PAIR "10's" VS. 6

	STAY	SPLIT
W	806	1006
P	110	97
L	84	480
UR	1722	1526

STAY PAIR "10's" VS. 6

9 VS. 2

	HIT	DOUBLE
W	494	920
P	80	72
L	426	936
UR	1068	984

HIT 9 VS. 2

8 VS. 5

	HIT	**DOUBLE**	**SPLIT "4's"**
W	512	952	1288
P	88	64	12
L	400	920	1352
UR	1112	1032	936

HIT 8 VS. 5

8 VS. 6

	HIT	DOUBLE	SPLIT "4's"
W	522	974	1259
P	63	44	39
L	415	938	1253
UR	1107	1036	1006

HIT 8 VS. 6

PAIR "9's" VS. 2

	STAY	SPLIT
W	505	999
P	135	145
L	360	789
UR	1145	1210

SPLIT PAIR "9's" VS. 2

According to my calculations based on Real World conditions, this is the Basic Strategy I recommend, and that I use myself. It is based on the most common Blackjack rules that I have found in the Casino's I have worked or played at. The rules are: a six deck shoe, dealer hits a soft"17", doubles down on any two cards, can split up to four hands, doubling after a split allowed, and Blackjack pays 3 to 2. I believe this is a solid Basic Strategy that can be used as a foundation in any Blackjack situation. If you are playing at a Casino with a large discrepancy from these rules, you could always go to the internet and see if there is a strategy with which you would feel more comfortable.

DEALER'S UPCARD

	2	3	4	5	6	7	8	9	10	ACE
8	H	H	H	H	H	H	H	H	H	H
9	H	D	D	D	D	H	H	H	H	H
10	D	D	D	D	D	D	D	H	H	H
11	D	D	D	D	D	D	D	D	D	H
12	H	H	S	S	S	H	H	H	H	H
13	S	S	S	S	S	H	H	H	H	H
14	S	S	S	S	S	H	H	H	H	H
15	S	S	S	S	S	H	H	H	H	H
16	S	S	S	S	S	H	H	H	H	H
A2	H	H	H	D	D	H	H	H	H	H
A3	H	H	H	D	D	H	H	H	H	H
A4	H	H	D	D	D	H	H	H	H	H
A5	H	D	D	D	D	H	H	H	H	H
A6	H	D	D	D	D	H	H	H	H	H
A7	S	D	D	D	D	S	S	H	H	H
A8	S	S	S	S	S	S	S	S	S	S
A9	S	S	S	S	S	S	S	S	S	S
AA	SP	SP	SP	SP	SP	SP	SP	SP	SP	SP
22	SP	SP	SP	SP	SP	SP	H	H	H	H
33	SP	SP	SP	SP	SP	SP	H	H	H	H
44	H	H	H	H	H	H	H	H	H	H
66	SP	SP	SP	SP	SP	H	H	H	H	H
77	SP	SP	SP	SP	SP	SP	H	H	H	H
88	SP	SP	SP	SP	SP	SP	SP	SP	SP	SP
99	SP	SP	SP	SP	SP	S	SP	SP	S	S
XX	S	S	S	S	S	S	S	S	S	S

PLAYER'S TWO CARD HAND

H: HIT   D: DOUBLE
S: STAY   SP: SPLIT

Another variable that the Casino may offer is "surrender". This means that after you have received your first two cards, and the dealer doesn't have Blackjack, you may surrender your hand. You will lose one half your bet and your hand is over. Many players say "If the casino offers this, it must not be good for the players". In fact there are several situations where it is advantageous for the player to surrender. If you have a two card total of "16" vs. a dealer's "9,10, Ace" you should surrender. The exception to this is that if your "16" was composed of a pair of "8's", you should split and not surrender. You should also surrender a "15" vs. "10" and a "17" vs. "Ace".

Also, you should never take insurance when the Dealer is showing an Ace. You should also not take "even money" when you have a Blackjack and the Dealer is showing an Ace. You will not maximize your winnings by making these two decisions.

I cannot encourage you enough to consistently play a solid Basic Strategy hand in and hand out.

From my twenty years of observation, my own playing experience, and my research, this is the foundation for winning more and losing less during your Blackjack playing sessions.

As explained earlier, my Real World Basic Strategy will differ slightly from one of the most common Basic Strategy charts. The differences are: you should hit a pair of "4's" against a dealers "5" or "6", not split; you should hit a "10" vs. "9" not double; and you should double a soft "16" vs. a "3", not just hit.

Here is the most common Basic Strategy chart that I have encountered over the years, in the best Blackjack books I have read. You can compare the two charts and see the several differences I suggest when you encounter Real World conditions.

DEALER'S UPCARD

	2	3	4	5	6	7	8	9	10	ACE
8	H	H	H	H	H	H	H	H	H	H
9	H	D	D	D	D	H	H	H	H	H
10	D	D	D	D	D	D	D	D	H	H
11	D	D	D	D	D	D	D	D	D	H
12	H	H	S	S	S	H	H	H	H	H
13	S	S	S	S	S	H	H	H	H	H
14	S	S	S	S	S	H	H	H	H	H
15	S	S	S	S	S	H	H	H	H	H
16	S	S	S	S	S	H	H	H	H	H
A2	H	H	H	D	D	H	H	H	H	H
A3	H	H	H	D	D	H	H	H	H	H
A4	H	H	D	D	D	H	H	H	H	H
A5	H	H	D	D	D	H	H	H	H	H
A6	H	D	D	D	D	H	H	H	H	H
A7	S	D	D	D	D	S	S	H	H	H
A8	S	S	S	S	S	S	S	S	S	S
A9	S	S	S	S	S	S	S	S	S	S
AA	SP	SP	SP	SP	SP	SP	SP	SP	SP	SP
22	SP	SP	SP	SP	SP	SP	H	H	H	H
33	SP	SP	SP	SP	SP	SP	H	H	H	H
44	H	H	H	SP	SP	H	H	H	H	H
66	SP	SP	SP	SP	SP	H	H	H	H	H
77	SP	SP	SP	SP	SP	SP	H	H	H	H
88	SP	SP	SP	SP	SP	SP	SP	SP	SP	SP
99	SP	SP	SP	SP	SP	S	SP	SP	S	S
XX	S	S	S	S	S	S	S	S	S	S

PLAYER'S TWO CARD HAND

H: HIT
S: STAY

D: DOUBLE
SP: SPLIT

Here is another interesting chart that I developed from my research. It shows on average how many times a dealer will break or make a particular hand depending on his up card. One of the things I find interesting is that when a dealer shows a "7,8,9,10,or Ace", the dealer will make a hand and not break about 75% of the time. There is not just much difference between a dealer showing a "7" or a "10".

There is a high probability that the dealer will make a hand. Many times a player will be more apt to stay on certain hands that they should hit, when a dealer shows a "7". The thinking is that unless the dealer has a "10" or an "Ace" in the hole, the dealer will have to draw and will break. This is just not the case. You must hit your hand against a "7" according to Basic Strategy.

PERCENTAGE OF TIME DEALER WILL MAKE A TOTAL

DEALER'S UPCARD

HAND RESULT		2	3	4	5	6	7	8	9	10	ACE
	BJ	-	-	-	-	-	-	-	-	8	31
	BUST	36	38	40	42	44	26	24	23	23	20
	17	13	13	12	12	12	37	13	12	12	8
	18	14	13	13	12	12	14	36	12	12	21
	19	13	13	12	12	12	8	13	35	12	21
	20	13	12	12	11	11	8	7	12	37	21
	21	12	12	11	11	11	7	7	6	4	10

JOHN LUCAS

CHAPTER 3

Real World Progressive Betting Strategy

NOW THAT THE proper Real World Basic Strategy has been determined, the next area to look at is how much to bet. Is it best to only bet the same flat amount each bet? Is it advantageous to increase ones bet when on a winning streak, and if so, when should one increase their bet and by how much? Some players are "negative" bettors. They like to increase their after they have lost three, four, or more hands in a row. They believe it must be their time to win and try and recapture their losses from their previous few bets.

My analysis of different betting strategies was determined by dealing myself approximately 200,000 hands of Blackjack, and playing these hands using my Real World Basic Strategy. These 200,000 hands were played under Real World conditions of people jumping in and out of shoes, some players playing a solid Basic Strategy while others playing poorly. Some shoes were one on one with the dealer, while other shoes had a variety of number of players. I then analyzed the strings of wins and losses and determined if there was a Betting System that would allow you to consistently gain an advantage, either in the long term or in the short term, over the Casino. Betting Strategies were analyzed in the long term by looking at the totality of the 200,000 hands. It was also analyzed in the short term by looking at results after a certain number of shoes, for instance, what does the analysis look like after 6, 8, 10, 20, etc shoes.

In the next chapter of Money Management, I will discuss further the guidelines for how much to buy in for, what your initial flat bet should be, and when you should leave the Casino whether ahead or behind.

I analyzed my results using twenty of the most common betting strategies I have observed in my many years of dealing. The basis of my analysis was charting the wins/losses by just using a flat bet throughout the entire 200,000 hands. I then analyzed the wins/losses by using the most common progressive betting systems I have witnessed. A few but not all are:

1). Increase your bet one unit after every win. Once a loss occurs you return to betting one unit. Here is an example of winning five hands in a row and then losing the sixth hand. The number stands for the betting unit, while the (W) stands for winning the hand, and the (L) means the hand was lost. 1(W), 2(W), 3(W), 4(W), 5(W), 6(L), 1 etc. As you can see that after winning the first hand at one betting unit, the second had was increased to 2 betting units and so on. On the sixth hand in which 6 units were bet there was a loss, so the pattern began again with betting one unit.

2). You bet a flat bet until you win two in a row. You then increase your bet by one unit after every two wins. When a loss occurs, you return to one betting unit. Example 1(W), 1(W), 2(W), 2(W), 3(W), 3(W), 4(W), 4(W), etc until you lose.

3). Bet one unit and if you win, bet two units, then go back to one unit and keep this pattern up. Once a loss occurs start at one unit. Example 1(W), 2(W), 1(W), 2(W), etc.

4). After one win go to three units bet and if won go back to one unit. Example 1(W), 3(W), 1(W), 3(W), etc. if a loss occurs, always return to one unit bet. These last two patterns are in a sense pocketing some profit after every two wins.

5). Stacking or parlaying your bets for three wins in a row and then returning to one unit bet. Any loss along the way and you start again with betting one unit. Example 1(W), 2(W), 4(W), 1(W), etc.

6). Parlaying your bet for four wins in a row before returning to one bet. Example 1(W), 2(W), 4(W), 8(W), 1(W), etc.

I looked at many other progressive betting patterns. I also looked at several "negative" betting patterns, that a player will increase their bet after they have lost two, three, four, or more hands in a row. Most players I have observed have a betting pattern, and if you do, I probably analyzed your pattern or something close to it. Of course, there are some players that seem to raise and lower their bets haphazardly. One player I have dealt to comes to mind. He sometimes increases his bet when he is losing, sometimes when he is winning. His increases don't follow any pattern, and no, he is not a card counter. He plays a decent Basic Strategy, but his bets are all over the place. He also plays fairly big money, with his bets fluctuating between $50 to $500. The result is that I know he loses about $100,000 a year. He can afford it, but it does show me that even if you play a decent Basic Strategy but your Betting Strategy is weak, you are not going to be a winning Blackjack player.

After the final analysis, what did I determine to be the best betting pattern to either lose less in the long run, or consistently gain an advantage and get ahead in the short run. It may surprise you that if one looks at the win/loss results over the total 200,000 hands played under Real World conditions, the best bet was to always bet a flat bet of the same amount. You will lose money, but significantly less than many of the other betting patterns I charted. Do I propose that you should only bet a flat amount each hand? The answer is no. Even though over the long term, flat betting will allow you to lose less than any other betting system, we don't play Blackjack to lose, rather to win. What if one looks at more reasonable playing sessions of one, two, or three hours? Is there another pattern that will limit your losses to a minimum, similar to a flat betting strategy, but will increase your bankroll during a winning streak? The answer is, yes.

Let's face it, every conservative betting player that has experienced a long winning streak of seven, eight, nine, or more hands in a row feels disappointed, when looking back, that they didn't increase their bets more aggressively during the streak. The majority of shoes are "choppy", meaning that the wins and losses occur in groups of two or three. This means that you may lose two or three hands before you win or conversely win two or three hands before you lose. It's a back and forth affair. The problem I see and charted with most progressive systems, especially with choppy shoes, is that when you increase your bet semi-aggressively or very aggressively and even though you may win three, four, or five hands in a row, when the loss does occur, that a majority of the time you lose a bet with a significant number of units bet and you would have ended up with more units by just flat betting. In, fact I have seen time and time again, that a player who increases their bets continually after several winning hands and then lose a double down, actually end up with significantly less units than if they had just bet a flat amount during the winning streak. Not only do they end up with less units, they actually have a negative unit loss, while the flat bettor would have shown a positive unit gain.

How about the negative betting systems, which means that you increase your bet after losing a number of hands, with the hope that you will win back your losses in one winning hand. Some people use the Martingale betting system where you keep doubling your bet after every loss. When you do win you will be ahead by the original amount you first bet. Here is an example of this betting system that shows losing five hands in a row before winning the sixth hand. It would look like this, with the numbers representing the units bet, and the (L) and (W) meaning loss or win. 1(L), 2(L), 4(L), 8(L), 16(L), 32(W). In this scenario, by the sixth hand you would be betting 32 units. If you were $10 player this would be $320, and when you won this sixth bet, you would be up only one unit or $10. I find this mindset of betting $320 to win $10 illogical. In fact if the player lost this sixth bet, they would have to bet $640 on the next hand. In many Casinos this would be over the tables limit, and you would not be able to make this bet. I do see some people use this system to some degree. I have occasionally seen it work when the shoes are choppy and the player never loses more than three, four, or five in a row. In my observations and from my 200,000 hand analysis, this is a very bad betting pattern in the short and long run.

Other players use a variation of this where they will only increase their bet after losing three, four, or five in a row. They feel that it must be "their turn to win". From what I have seen, this type of negative betting pattern is more common than the Martingale system. This does work sometimes during some playing sessions, but overall, any of the "bet more to catch up" betting systems just don't hold up. This is from personal observation and my analysis I conducted in the writing of this book.

So if many of the progressive betting systems produce overall worse results than just making a flat bet every hand, and the negative betting systems are even worse, did I find a system that does work. The answer is yes. The betting system I recommend and use successfully myself is a conservative progressive betting system that accomplishes three things:

1). Over the long term of the 200,000 hands I dealt using Real World conditions, it came in a close second to the flat betting system in terms of minimizing total losses.

2). In the shorter term, when looking at Real World playing sessions of one, two, or three hours and playing in choppy shoes where there were few very long winning or losing streaks, my betting system normally held up to or surpassed the flat betting system. It didn't fall into the trap of many progressive betting systems in which the player raises his bet too aggressively and when a loss occurs, especially if this loss is a double down, the player actually would have ended up with more units if they had been using a flat bet.

3). During a long winning streak this system becomes increasingly aggressive and will gain a nice profit.

The good thing about this system is that even if you lose a sizable bet during a winning streak, you will still be significantly ahead and will have a nice gain in your bankroll. I call my betting system the Real World Progressive Betting System. Now let's analyze this in more detail.

This is how my Real World Progressive Betting System works. Let's consider how when using this system you would bet if you won sixteen hands in a row. OK, I know that this long of a winning streak is rare, although it does happen. I want to show you this so that you grasp the progressive betting pattern I recommend. I will then show you how you can get to the higher betting units when winning streaks occur, but less than the sixteen in a row I am showing. The "number" is the betting units for the hand. The (W) or (L) shows whether you won or loss that particular hand. We will look at a sixteen hand winning streak that does not contain any doubles or splits. Here it is: 1(W), 1(W), 1(W), 2(W), 2(W), 3(W), 3(W), 5(W), 5(W), 7(W), 7(W), 10(W), 10(W), 15(W), 15(W), 20(W). As you can see using the Real World Progressive Betting System, you must initially win three hands in a row at one betting unit before increasing to two betting units. After these first three wins, you then must win two hands in a row before you increase your betting units to the next level. Initially you will only increase your betting unit by one unit as you win. Once you win two in a row at the three unit level, you will then jump to five units. As you can see that if you win two in a row at seven betting units, you will jump up to ten units and if you continue to win, you increase by five units to betting fifteen and then twenty units. This system starts out conservatively but gets progressively more aggressive as the wins continue. Any time during this streak that you should lose, you start back at betting one unit.

Now let's look at some fine tuning of the system that shows how you can get to the higher betting units without winning sixteen hands in a row. This will depend on the doubling and splitting hands you win. Except for the first three hands, where I recommend betting one unit for three winning hands until you start to increase your betting units, you will count a winning doubling or splitting hand as winning two hands and will jump ahead to the next level. Let's see how that after winning the first three hands how a winning doubling hand will effect your betting units progression. When you win a double this will be signified by the symbols (WD). 1(W), 1(W), 1(W), 2(WD), 3(WD), 5(W), 5(W), 7(WD), 10. Here is a scenario where you get to the ten betting units level by only winning eight hands in a row as opposed to having to win eleven in a row with no doubling wins. In this example, after getting to the two betting units level and you win a double, you then jump ahead to the three betting units level. If you win a double at this level, you jump ahead to the five betting units level. This betting systems says that that a double or split win counts as two wins and you should jump ahead in your betting units as the previously laid out Real World Progressive Betting System dictates. If you get a Blackjack during your winning progression, only count this as a one unit win and don't jump ahead in your betting. If you encounter a splitting situation where you may split up to three or four hands and even have some doubles on some or all of these hands, you could in effect win six, seven, or eight units in one hand. Only count this as two wins in jumping ahead in the Real World Progressive Betting System. For example, what if you were at the three unit betting level and you had a hand where you split up to three hands with a double on each of these three hands. In this case, you would win six units on this one hand. On your next bet, only bet five units, don't jump to the seven unit level.

I am now going to look at more closely on how to bet when you win doubling or splitting hands during the first three hands when you are betting one unit. If you win a double or split during the first or second hand when you are betting your initial one unit, do not count these as two wins and jump ahead to the two betting unit level. For example, 1(W), 1(WD), 1(W), 2. Even though you won a double in the second hand, do not jump ahead to the two betting unit level on the third hand. Continue to bet one unit on the third hand and if you win this, then move on to the two unit betting level. The exception to this is that if you win a double or splitting hand on the first two hands that you are betting one unit, then on the third hand jump ahead to the two betting unit level. It would look like this, 1(WD), 1(WD), 2.

Very long winning streaks where you get to ten or more winning hands in a row does happen but is not common. Winning streaks of five or six hands in a row are obviously much more common. Let us look at six hand winning streak that contains some doubles and compare my Real World Progressive Betting System to a flat betting system. Here is the scenario: 1(WD), 1(WD), 2(W), 2(W), 3(WD), 5(W), 5(L). In this case, because you won some doubling hands during this six hand winning streak, you jumped ahead in your betting progression until you lost a five unit bet. If you were a $10 player and were using Real World Progressive Betting System, this would have resulted you being up by $190 until you lost a $50 on the five unit bet. The result is a $140 gain for this six hand winning streak. A flat unit bettor would have had a net gain $80. During this short winning streak, the Real World Progressive Betting System would have had a $60 gain over a flat betting strategy.

In this particular scenario, a $25 player would have profited $350 and a $150 gain over a flat unit bettor. A $100 player would have profited $1,400 and a $600 gain over a player that uses a flat bet. Even when the loss occurred at the five unit bet, and if this loss had been a double down bet which in this scenario would have been a $100 loss for a $10 player, the player using the Real World Progressive Betting Strategy would have still had a greater profit when compared to a player that was using a flat betting strategy.

Let me sum up The Real World Progressive Betting System analysis. As stated earlier, the overall best betting system over the long term to lose less is just to always place the same flat bet. If you use a flat betting system, this is actually not a bad way to bet. You can play a long while on a modest buy in, and even get ahead of the Casino for short periods of time. I will discuss further in the next chapter of Money Management of when a player should take their winnings and leave the Casino. If you continually quit playing when you are ahead, you can actually make a small amount of profit quite consistently using a flat betting system. Of course over the long term, if you never quit playing, you would always lose money no matter what type of betting system you used. From my calculations and observation of many of the most common progressive and negative betting systems that are used, I recommend using my Real World Progressive Betting System. That is because over a very long period of continual play your losses will be minimized when compared with using a flat betting system. Since most people play for shorter playing sessions, which is what I will recommend in the Money Management chapter, my Real World Progressive Betting System has several advantages. In the very long term this system will be comparable to a flat betting system in terms of reducing your losses. The upside is that the Real World Progressive Betting System will, in the short run, minimize your losses when the cards are not going your way, but your wins will be maximized when you are on a longer winning streak or even during choppy streaks. When I play, this is the system I use, and as I will detail later, my winning sessions outnumber my losing sessions and overall I make a profit.

I have now detailed two of the three areas in my Real World Blackjack System. The first one was Real World Basic Strategy that shows how you should play each hand of Blackjack that you will encounter. The second was the Real World Progressive Betting System, that details how much you should bet on winning and losing streaks. The following chapter pertains to Money Management. All three are equally important if you want to lay the foundation of playing winning Blackjack.

CHAPTER 4

Real World Money Management

T HE THIRD LEG in learning how to play winning Blackjack is in the area of Money Management. This is normally not the most exciting area to talk about, but it is as crucial as the other two areas of Basic Strategy and Betting Strategies. The fact is, no matter how you bet or how much you get ahead, it means nothing if you don't know when to take your profits and leave. I have seen thousands of times that a player will get significantly ahead in a short or medium amount of time but continue to stay for hours as their profits dwindle and they eventually leave the Casino not ahead, but even very far behind. Perhaps some of the readers of this book has seen this happen to themselves. I have also seen thousands of times a player who is on a losing streak that just keeps pulling money out of his pocket, or ATM, in the hopes of getting on a winning streak in the hopes of getting their money back. Of course, sometimes this does work, but in the majority of time, the player will lose many times over the amount they had budgeted for. This reminds me of a specific player who played fairly large amounts of $100 to $500 a hand on either one or two hands at a time. He would often get behind six or seven thousand dollars, but would keeping getting more and even betting more aggressively. Over a period of a month, this did seem to work. He seemed to eventually get his money back, and even get head, sometimes significantly. Eventually it caught up to him. Over a several weeks period, he just couldn't make a comeback, with the result of him losing $10,000 or more each session. He finally quit coming to my Casino, and I know his total losses were in the $75,000 range. I have seen this time and time again, though normally on a smaller scale.

The two areas of Real World Money Management I will be discussing are: 1)How long to play and 2) Setting losing and winning limits. I found through personal observation, my own personal playing experience, and as a result of analyzing over 200,00 hands, that both of these areas are very significant if you want to play winning Blackjack. By sticking to certain guidelines, I believe you can consistently walk out of a Casino with a profit. From my perspective, the overall all reason to play Blackjack is to Win.

The first area to discuss is setting a time limit for your playing session. This somewhat pertains to the players who live close to a Casino or number of Casinos and gambles on a somewhat regular basis. I see many players who come into the Casino on almost a daily basis for some period of time, and if they don't come to the Casino in which I work, they tell me they that they also go to other Casinos in the area on a regular basis. For players that regularly frequent Casinos, then it is my experience that setting a time limit for your playing session is crucial if you want to consistently win at Blackjack. If you are a player that only plays occasionally or visits Casinos on your vacations, then setting a time limit may not pertain to you. In these cases, you will probably going to be playing Blackjack for much longer periods within a shorter period of time. I would still recommend you use My Real World Basic Strategy and my Real World Progressive Betting System. I believe you will win more and lose less during your longer playing sessions.

Now let's look at setting time limits. If you are a regular player that is serious about being a winner time limits are essential. I determined these guidelines from twenty years of personal observation and also by playing and charting thousands of hands and shoes. As I stated before, I played over 200,000 hands of Blackjack using my Basic Strategy and my Betting System using Real World conditions. I not only charted the win/loss results over the total 200,000 hands, but also broke it down to the wins and losses per shoe. Added to this equation, is the losing and winning limit guidelines which I discuss in more detail in the coming paragraphs.

The time limit I recommend is either around 1 ½ hours or about six to seven shoes. At this point you should either take your winnings (there will be an exception to this to be discussed later) or absorb your losses, even if its only a few dollars either way. The reason that I picked this time limit is because from the regular players I observe that use this time limit and aren't even using a great Basic Strategy or Betting Strategy, they seem to over time stay about even with the Casino or lose very little over a years time. I even know a few, that over the course of a particular year, even come out ahead. I believe that if they had been using a better Basic Strategy or Betting System, they would have actually increased their winnings even more. By limiting themselves to this time limit, they have limited their losses, and yes have also possibly limited their winnings. They have avoided the unavoidable fact that the longer you play, the greater chances that your losses will increase. I also determined from charting thousands of shoes, that a player will at some point, a majority of the time, during the first six or seven shoes get ahead to some degree. The longer you play, the majority of the time this will mean the greater chances of losing and this initial gain will be lost.

There are exceptions, and I will detail how to adjust the time limit when these exceptions occur. If you should lose your "loss limit" (which will be detailed shortly) in a shorter period of time, you should leave the Casino and resist the temptation to buy in again in the hopes of getting your money back. The majority of the time, you will lose more by continuing to buy in for more chips. If you should achieve your "win limit" (to be detailed shortly) within this 1 ½ hour time limit, and then start to lose, you should then leave the Casino and enjoy your profit. Another exception that I will detail later is that if you should reach your "win limit" but you continue to win, you will play beyond this 1 ½ time limit. When this occurs you should keep on playing as you continue to win. Never quit while on a winning streak. I will discuss shortly when to raise your "winning limit" when a winning streak occurs, and then when to leave when losses start to occur.

The second area of Real World Money Management involves how much you should buy in for, which will determine your "win/loss limits". What kind of player you are, whether a $5, $10, $25, or $100 player depends on your own personal finances and your gambling personality. These amounts reflect what will be your starting unit amount when using the Real World Progressive Betting System. All that I can do is strongly advise is that you play within your financial means. Depending on what kind of player you are will determine what kind of winning goals and losing limits you should set for yourself. To play consistent winning Blackjack, you have to know when to take your profit and leave and conversely, how much to lose before leaving.

The Real World Money Management system suggests that you buy in for twenty units of whatever type of betting player you are. If you are a $5 player, you will buy in for $100. A $10 player should buy in for $200, a $25 player for $500, and a $100 player for $2,000. If you are a player that likes to play two hands and let's say you are playing $10 on each hand, then your buy in will be $400. This twenty unit buy in will determine your "win/loss" limits.

Let me first talk about your loss limit. If you are a $5 player, you will buy in for $100. You start playing the Real World Progressive Betting System with a $5 bet. If you should lose your $100 buy in within the 1 ½ hour time limit,you should leave and resist the urge to buy in for more. From my calculations, that if you play Real World Basic Strategy and use the Real World Progressive Betting System, the chances of losing all twenty units within the suggested playing time is rare. It does occasionally happen, but it is uncommon to lose all twenty units. From my calculations, you will only lose all twenty units once or twice per thirty playing sessions within the playing time limit. Assuming you don't lose the total buy in within the playing time limit, you should then leave the Casino after your 1 ½ hour time limit has been reached no matter losses look like. It may be a $75, $50, $25, or even only a $10 loss, but when the time limit is reached, within a few minutes either way, I suggest you leave with your remaining funds. Even leaving with small amounts of money adds up over many playing sessions. What if after the time limit you had only $25 left of your initial $100 buy in? It is easy to try and stick around longer and play this $25 and sometimes this may work. A majority of the time you will lose this $25. Let's say over a years worth of play this happened twenty times. By leaving with this $25, you will have kept $500 more in your bankroll. Small amounts of winnings or losses add up over the long term.

Now let's look at having a "winning limit" goal. I suggest that you set up your goal to be 70% of your buy in. For a $5 player with a $100 buy in, the goal would be to win $70. A $10 players goal would be $140, a $25 players goal would be $350, and a $100 player would have a winning goal of $1,400. Let's say you don't reach your goal within the suggested playing time limit. In this case, once time has expired, you should leave the Casino with whatever winnings you have. Maybe you are only $10, $25, or $50 ahead. You should then leave with your winnings.

If during the time limit you reach your winning goal, when should you leave? My research suggests that once your winning goal has been met and then you start losing, you should then leave. If you were a $5 player with a winning goal of $70 and after a few shoes you were up by $80 or $85, you should then leave once losses start to occur. Once you have dropped back down to $65 or $70, you should then leave the Casino, only if you have been playing for a ½ hour. You have reached your goal and you had started losing, so have the discipline to leave with your winnings. I realize people want to "win big" and at times this will happen, but to be a consistent winning Blackjack player, don't be ashamed of collecting a number of smaller wins. They do significantly add up.

Let's look at how consistent small wins can add up over a period of time. From my calculations, a player will be up 30% of their buy in at least 8 out of 10 times they play within the 1 ½ hour time limit. This means that a $5 player will up at least $30 at some point during a majority of his playing sessions within the playing time limit. A $25 player would be up $150 and a $100 would be up at least $600 at some point during a majority of their playing sessions. Percentage wise, this is not a large amount, and I am not suggesting that you leave once you get 30% ahead, but let's look at how a number of consistent small wins can accumulate. Hypothetically, let's assume a player plays everyday of the year. Actually, this is not a big stretch for number of regular players. I know a number of regulars that play at least five or six days a week. Using the figures above, if a $5 player won $30 a day for a whole year, this would be $10,950. For a $25 player it would be $54,750, and for a $100 player that years total would be $219,000. So it is obvious that for someone who plays Blackjack a lot, and is content with a number of small wins, that these small wins can accumulate to a large amount of money.

Another scenario is that you get on a winning streak and that you easily reach your winning goal and then some. If you continue to win, keep playing even past the suggested time limit. A good winning streak is not something to be stopped. Never stop when a winning streak is in full force. Here is an example. After 1 ½ hours a $5 player is up $150. The player has been consistently winning shoe after shoe, but the time limit has been reached. The player should pocket $120 of profit and not spend any of this and continue to play with the remaining $30. If this $30 is lost, the player should leave with a $120 profit. If the player continues to win, they should pocket any winnings over the $30 and not touch this and keep playing. Now let's look at the possibility that you just keep winning, and how you could increase your basic $5 betting unit to $10. Still using this example, let's say the player continues to win and is now up $300. At this point, they could pocket $250 of profit and play with the remaining $50, but increase their base unit bet to $10 and continue to play using Real World Basic Strategy and Real World Progressive Betting. Pocket any wins over this $50 and keep playing. Once the $50 is gone, leave the Casino with a very nice profit. There are times where everything goes right and you continue to win shoe after shoe. It is somewhat rare, but it does happen. When it does, you must take advantage of it.

Several times I have had such a winning streak occur when I am playing. In my case, once I raised my basic unit of betting to $10, I just kept winning. At one point I was up $750 so I pocketed $650 of this and raised my basic betting unit to $25. Since I only had $100 to play with at playing $25 a hand, I didn't really expect it to last much longer. To my surprise, I consistently kept winning. I got up to $1,350 ahead, so I pocketed $1,150 of this and played with the remaining $200. I then raised my basic betting unit to $50. At this point it went back an forth until I lost the $200, at which point I left with $1,150 profit. When a winning streak like this does occur, it definitely covers many of the losing sessions that have been experienced. As I will explain in the following chapter, where I detail several of my "30 playing sessions" gambling experiences, where I had more winning than losing sessions, this $1,150 win more than offset all my losses for this particular "30 session" playing period. One reason for this is since I follow my loss limit and time limit guidelines, when I did lose, my average losses were not overly significant.

To sum up this chapter and the previous two chapters, I believe that you can win more than you lose over a period of time playing Blackjack. You must be disciplined and have a long view. You must Manage your Money wisely, play a good Basic Strategy hand in and hand out, and you must have a winning Betting Strategy. I believe my Real World analysis in these areas, if followed, can help you be a winning Blackjack player. I realize there are no guarantees, but I challenge you to absorb what I have suggested, and then follow these suggestions for a thirty sessions of play, and chart your results. I have done this over several "30 playing sessions" and have come out ahead with a decent profit.

CHAPTER 5

My Real World Playing Sessions

U NTIL I DEVELOPED my Real World Strategies I used to play Blackjack in a hit or miss fashion, especially when it came time to leave the Casino. As many others, sometimes I stayed too long when ahead and sometimes when behind, I kept buying in to try and catch up. I didn't really have a plan and therefore didn't maximize my potential for winning. After doing my research, I decided to put it to the test in the Real World. I decided to play in groups of thirty "playing sessions" and chart my results. I religiously followed my Real World Basic Strategy, Real World Progressive Betting System, and my Real World Money Management guidelines.

My first thirty sessions of play was spread out over about two months. Since I have a number of Casinos within driving distance, I played these sessions at four different Casinos. By playing at number of different Casinos it would give truer Real World results. All of the Blackjack I played was with six deck shoes. I tended to go to casinos at times that weren't overly crowded. It is just in my nature that I don't enjoy very crowded environments. I would say on average I played with two other players. Sometimes I played one on one for an extended period of time, while at other times the tables were full. In these first thirty playing sessions I was a basic $5 player and bought in for $100. Here are the results.

Over these thirty sessions I had twenty winning sessions, one push, and nine losing sessions. My nine losing sessions were of the following amounts: $100, $90, $80, $75, $55, $30, $30, $10, and $5 for a total loss of $475. I averaged $53 per losing session. I attribute the average low losses to my Money Management guidelines and my Real World Progressive Betting System that is conservative at the beginning of play, which results in lower losses during a bad playing session. If I had bet more aggressively, I believe my losses would have been much greater. My twenty winning session were as follows: $1,150 (which I detailed in the last chapter), $375, $175, $135, three at $80, five at $60, three at $40, two at $30, two at $20, and one at $10. The total of my winning sessions was $2,605. The net profit for all thirty session was $2,130 or an average of $71 per session.

The shortest time I played was twenty minutes. After two shoes, I was up $95, and when it dropped down to $80 I left. My longest session was when I won $1,150 where I played for about three hours. I also played over my 1 ½ hour limit when I won $375, but overall I stuck with my 1 ½ hour time limit, especially when I was losing.

This $71 average win per session may not sound that great, but if projected out and I was playing $25 as my basic betting unit, this would translate to $355 per session or a total of $10,650, and if I was a $100 player, it would have been $1,420 per session or a total of $42,600 for the thirty sessions.

Of course there is no guarantees that this winning percentage would keep up. I then did another "thirty session play". This took place over four months, and I raised my basic betting unit to $10. My buy in was $200 and my "winning limit goal" was $140. During these thirty session I had twelve losing sessions and eighteen winning sessions. Only once did I lose the total $200 buy in. My average loss per losing session was $110 with a total loss of $1,320 for the twelve losing sessions. My average win per winning session was $140, with a total win of $2,520. My net win for all sessions was $1,200.

I next charted only twelve sessions of play. This time I bought in for $500 and raised my basic betting unit to $25. I won in eight sessions and lost in four. My average loss for my losing sessions was $250 per session with a total loss of $1,000. My total win for the eight winning sessions was $5,550. I netted $4,550 or an average win of $379 per session over the total twelve sessions. I did have two really good wins, one for $2,250 and another for $1,500. My lowest win was $50. I religiously followed my Real World Basic Strategy, my Real World Progressive Betting System, and Real World Money Management guidelines. Except for two sessions in which I extended my playing time because I was winning, I stuck with my 1 ½ hour playing limit.

Since I was up $7,880 for these three playing group sessions, I decided to do a few more session with my basic betting unit being $100. To bet this amount of money is definitely out of my comfort zone. I thought it would be interesting to see if I had the discipline to follow my Real World System. I charted ten session of play. My buy in for each of these ten session was $2,000. The results were as follows. I won in six playing sessions, and lost in four. My losses were of $2,000, $1,200, $550, and $150. My wins consisted of $2,400, $1,800, $900, $550, $425, and $100. My net profit was $2,275. I never played over 1 ½ hours. My shortest playing time was 45 minutes when I lost my total $2,000 buy in. Even though I played at a couple of different tables during this time, I just didn't win very many hands. Some days this will happen. The tables are just cold. Overall I was happy with the results. I must admit that it was somewhat nerve racking playing for these larger stakes, but I stuck to my system and came out ahead.

Since these four playing sessions that took about a year to complete, I continue to play sporadically. I continue to work at a Casino forty plus hours a week, and honestly don't really feel like gambling much in my off time. I am sure that when I retire, I will play Blackjack more regularly, but for now I only play when I really feel like it. It is satisfying to know that by using my Real World System, it has so far allowed me to win more than lose.

CHAPTER 6

Miscellaneous Casino Thoughts

LET ME MAKE some comments and observations on a number of areas involving Blackjack. These are things I have observed over the years about Blackjack, players, management, and other things that go on in the casino work environment.

Card Counting: Does card counting really work? Even though I am not 100% convinced it works that well, I must assume it does. This is because of the numerous books that have been and are continuing to be written about it. Every year there seem to be a more simpler and effective system written about that you can learn. This makes me wonder that if there is always new better systems coming out, maybe the old systems weren't that effective in the first place. If the old systems were that great, why do they need constant tweaking and improvement? Maybe the old systems were were OK, but just too hard to learn. Maybe the new systems are simpler and just as effective. Or, maybe people just want to sell more books, so they make minor changes to an existing card counting system.

There must be some merit in card counting because I know that the Casinos I have worked for get pictures and descriptions of suspected card counters when they have been spotted in the area. Supervisors and sometimes dealers are told to be on the look out for these individuals. If they do come to your table, the dealer has been instructed to cut the shoe so that the suspected card counter has very little of the shoe to play with. Sometimes the supervisor has been told not to deal to the card counter at all. He or she is told that while they can play any other Casino game, they won't be allowed to play Blackjack. Actually over the many years I have dealt, I have encountered very few known card counters. It is always possible that a few have slipped through without being recognized as card counters, but I believe this would be a very small number of players.

Overall, it seems that many of the card counting systems are just too complicated for the average person to learn, especially when most Casinos use a six deck shoe. Besides keeping track of the plus/minus count, the running count,and the true count, the player must learn many changes to Basic Strategy that occurs depending on the count. For the average player this probably is too much to learn. I have no interest in learning a card counting system, since my Real World System seems to, so far anyhow, worked for me very profitably. I do know there are some simpler type of card counting systems out there. I really don't know if they work or not, but I am satisfied with using the Real World System I have developed. It is not that hard to learn. The main thing it requires is discipline.

Casino Surveillance: How sharp really are the surveillance departments in many Casinos? I can only speak for the ones that I have observed. In terms of catching mistakes during a live game or figuring out if a player is a potential card counter, I don't believe that they are that effective. They are useful if a player or dealer believes that a mistake had just happened, and the supervisor will ask surveillance to "look at the tape". Normally, but not always, they can determine if a mistake occurred. In my twenty years of dealing, I have only had it happen once, where surveillance called down and said they saw where I had made a mistake on a live game. I consider myself to be an accurate dealer, but I am sure I have made more mistakes than this over my many years of dealing that was not caught. When it comes to card counting, from my experience surveillance is most used "after the fact". By this I mean that a player has won a substantial amount of money and his play seemed suspicious. Normally after they are gone, someone in surveillance, who has the proper training, will review the person's play to determine if they are some sort of "advantage" player. In the Casinos I have worked, there is normally only one or two people that are good enough to determine this, and I don't believe their expertise is foolproof. The rank and file surveillance workers are some of the lowest paid employees in the Casino. Many don't even have a good grasp of common Basic Strategy. Unless notified by the pit personnel, there is a good chance that they would never catch anything out of the ordinary going on.

Casino Supervisors: How qualified are the Pit Supervisors all the way up to the Shift Managers in a Casino? As in any organization, some are very sharp and knowledgeable, while others follow the The Peter Principle, where they have risen to their level of incompetence. The sharp ones know what's going on at every table. They know how each player is playing, whether they are playing Basic Strategy and how they are betting or varying their bets. A lot of Pit Supervisors spend a lot of time flirting with the cocktail staff or dealers on dead games. They may congregate and talk about sports for long periods of time. Many just talk about whatever drama is taking place in their life. These type generally don't have much of a clue on what's taking place at any table at any particular time.

If you were to give a nationwide test to Shift and Pit Supervisors on Basic strategy, there is no doubt in my mind that a majority would do very poorly on the test. Many are very short sighted and become overly suspicious of anyone new that happens to win some money. One Shift Manager that I have worked for, time and time again, becomes very nervous if someone new wins a decent amount of money and seems to play strangely. They are convinced that this player is "up to something" and will have surveillance later review the tapes to try and figure it out. What has happened in every case, is that the individual will continue to come back and play and end up losing a lot of money. Their "strange play" was just that, strange. They basically were playing and betting by intuition, and had just happened to occasionally get lucky. This Shift Manager doesn't pay attention to how the player is following or not following Basic Strategy, or really paying attention to the betting pattern the player is using. All this Manager knows is that here is someone new and he is playing oddly and is winning. Many times if the Dealers were asked (heaven forbid that the Dealers may have some insight), they could tell the Manager that they had seen this player a number of times and could detail how they think they play. Rarely is a Dealer, even a sharp one, asked about a particular player. All that is looked at is that player is winning and playing strangely, so let the panic begin. Also, the truth is that you'd be surprised how many Shift and Pit Supervisors have never even dealt the games they are supervising.

How does the Pit Personnel react to someone who is winning big money? It really depends on the particular Shift Manager on duty. Some really "sweat the money" and will continually change Dealers in hopes of finding one who will turn the tide. The may even instruct the Dealer to change the way they shuffle. These type may even degrade the Dealer because he or she is losing. Even when these Managers have been told by higher ups to loosen up and just let the odds play out, they just can't seem to let it go. These are not enjoyable Supervisors to work under. Most of the

Shift or Pit Supervisors I have worked under are not this type. They realize that people win big sometimes and in the long run, the Casino will come out ahead.

Life of a Dealer: What's it like to be a Casino Dealer? If you like to play games and interact with people, it's a very enjoyable job. The pay can vary greatly. If you work in a small casino in some out of the way area, you may only make around $20,000 to $25,000. If you work at high end Casino in Las Vegas, you can make upwards of $100,000. Most Dealers make something in between. There are drawbacks in being a Dealer. Many Dealers develop numerous physical ailments as feet, leg, and back problems. Many others get carpal tunnel symptoms. Long hours of standing in one place does take its toll. An egotistical Pit Supervisor can make your working day miserable if they don't like you. Working schedules can be less than desirable. They can constantly change to some degree week to week. You will probably have to work many Holidays. Some days you seem to attract every negative customer in the area. You have to learn to "hold your tongue" when such a customer is directly or indirectly aiming their negativity at you.

Overall, I found have Dealers to be good people with a good sense of humor. The break room is filled with jokes, ribbing, and laughter. Yes, we do have our share of complainers, but what work place doesn't? I must admit that the humor can be risque, many times bordering on sexual harassment or political incorrectness. Yes, Dealers do talk about you, the customer. We have our favorites and on the opposite side, there are players we hate to see come to our table. Trust me, if you are a player that wins and doesn't tip, or barely tips, the Dealers are definitely going to talk about you. If you are a player with a good personality and tips, you will also be talked about in a positive light. Dealers even have nicknames for many of the regulars. This is especially true for players that are not that well liked. Nicknames as Whiner, Vulture, The Stork, Surrender Sam, Smelly, Tightwad, Dickhead, Clueless, and many others that contain some degree of vulgarity come to mind.

Player Etiquette: They are some unwritten rules that Blackjack players should observe. One is that if you come to a Blackjack table in the middle of a shoe, you should ask the other players at the table if they want you to get in, or would they rather have you wait. Many players will just wait until the shoe is over and then start at the beginning of the new shoe. It is surprising how many players will rudely just enter a game in the middle of a shoe without asking.

Secondly, players that are on a losing streak should stop whining and complaining or throwing temper tantrums. This could be about how other players are playing their cards or even about the Dealer. Are they that ignorant that they really think that the Dealer has any control on how the cards come out. No matter how good or bad the other players are playing, in the long run it has no effect on whether you win or lose. If you don't like another player for any reason, maybe it's the way there are playing or maybe it's just their personality, then just go to another table. Just stop complaining. More than likely this is just your personality that is always complaining about everything in life. If you recognize yourself as a complainer, I suggest you get some mental health counseling. You will be happier, not to mention the others that have to deal with you.

Thirdly, in the same vain, don't be a player that is always telling others how to play. If a new player asks for help, by all means help them out, otherwise be quiet and play your own cards. In fact, in most cases, the player who is always giving advice is many times a poor player themselves. Don't be a player that feels the need to quote statistics every hand. Nobody wants to hear it, especially the Dealer who has heard it all a thousand times before.

Fourthly, make sure you tip the Dealer. You may put a tip out on a particular hand, you may just occasionally give the Dealer a tip, you may only tip when you are leaving, or you may do all three. Even though I have no statistics to back this up, I have noticed that the players who seem to win the most are positive, friendly players who are good tippers. Let's just say it's "good karma".

Avoid Cliches: As a Dealer I have heard certain phrases so often that it borders on threatening my sanity. Most players that repeat these over used cliches act like they are informing the world of a new truth they have just realized. We have all heard them over and over again, please stop. Here are a few. When a Dealer has a "2" as an upcard, someone will surely say, "you know a Dealer's "2" is like a wild card". When a player makes a dumb move and loses, they will say, "well, that's why they call it gambling". If there are a number of people at the table and the dealer is showing a break card, someone will surly say, "you know someone has to take a hit", so someone will then hit a "13" total against a dealers "6". I don't know where this "someone has to take a hit" came from, but please, let it go away. It makes no sense. Another is that when a Dealer shows an "Ace", someone that doesn't have a Blackjack will say "give me even money". This may have been funny the first time I heard it, but please, no more. There are more, but you get the idea.

Changing Your Luck: Sometimes you are at a table where the dealer just keeps winning hand after hand. There is no law that says you have to stay at one table and get punished. Many times if I lose seven or eight hands in a row, and I just don't have a good feeling about the table, I will move. Though I normally tend to stick with one table through its ups and downs, there are times to move on and resume play at another table. Instead of moving to another table, a player can just sit a few hands out in the hopes of changing things. This is OK. It's not like you are going to make anything worse.

Money Management Stories: In my Real World Money Management chapter, I stressed the importance of "leaving when you are ahead". This reminds of one customer that would come to the Casino about twice a week. I will call this customer SK. SK was not a big player. He usually bought in for $100 and only placed $5, $10, or maybe $15 bets. He played a conservative Basic Strategy. SK would always hit when he was suppose to, but was conservative when it came to splitting and doubling down. Overall, SK seemed to win and leave the Casino ahead a majority of the time. One particular Shift Manager was convinced that he was "up to something". He wasn't winning big, but just because he seemed to almost always leave a winner, he was viewed as suspicious. One time when he came to my table, the Shift Manager, who at this point had gotten to know SK better, asked him, "how is it that you always seem to win?" SK said said, "watch and I'll show you". He bought in for $100 and for his first bet he bet $25. He won this bet and then said, "color me up, I'm leaving". As he was leaving, he said to the Shift Manager, "that's how, you leave when you are ahead!" Of course, normally he would not have left at this point, but he was making a point.

I also stressed the importance of having a winning limit goal. This can be taken too literally. It reminds of a player that came regularly that I will call CS. CS bought in for $200 and was a $10 player. He stated his goal was to win $200 and then leave. He got up to being $190 ahead, and said, "if I win one more bet I am out of here". I had dealt to CS enough that I knew he would leave once he reached his goal. Well, he started to lose. When he lost this first $10 bet and now was still up $180, and told him this was still a good win and he should leave. CS was determined to get to the $200 goal. Long story short, he ended up losing the $190 he was ahead and eventually bought in for another $1,000 and lost all of this. His stubbornness turned a positive win into a fairly large loss.

Betting Strategy Story: I stressed in my Real World Betting Strategy chapter that in the long run a more conservative strategy is the best. I know that there are those players that being very aggressive is their nature. One player comes to mind that was a fairly large bettor who was a very aggressive bettor. I will call this player MG. MG seemed to have the goal to get to the table maximum as soon as possible. He would start with his one unit bet, which in his case was $200. If he won this bet he would stack it and add one more unit to this bet for a total of $600. If he won this bet, he would then bet $1,000. At this particular Casino, he was now betting the table maximum. It was a $100 to $1,000 table. Obviously, when a player bets this aggressively and gets on on winning streak they can make a big profit, and sometimes this will happen. Conversely, if the shoes are choppy and winning three hands in a row is a rarity, you are going to be always behind when losing this third hand. I saw this player lose much more than he ever won, though at times MG did have some big wins. One particular time, MG started off hot and was up $20,000. He kept playing and eventually the shoes had no more long winning streaks. He ended up losing $75,000. It reinforced in me the believe of "leaving when ahead", which he didn't do, and also that very aggressive play in the long run is very costly. MG also played with some of his friends that played equally aggressive. These were successful businessmen that probably got where they were by being extremely competitive and ego driven. Though these qualities may be good in business, I don't believe it translates well in the world of Blackjack. I know for a fact, that over a two year period, that several of these individuals lost a minimum of $250,000 during this time.

Non-Discrimination: In a world that still has its share of sexism, racism, religious discrimination, and other forms of "isms", I find it heartening that many of these so called "divides" many times seem to disappear among Blackjack players. One day I was dealing to a full tables of a very diverse group of players. There were men and women of every age group. There was Asians, Hispanics, Blacks, and Caucasians. Some appeared to be wealthy, while others probably not so much. Here was a group of people that under normal circumstances would not been together. But, here they were having a great time. They were giving each other "high fives" (yes, they were all winning). There was good-natured banter between them, laughter, and overall they were having a great time. It dawned on me that this really doesn't happen that much. I guess the common goal of winning at Blackjack brought them together. I have noticed this many times since. I have seen friendships develop between people that would have probably never have met or interacted much if it wasn't for Blackjack. One friendship comes to mind between a very wealthy businessman and a younger minority lad. The businessman dresses in a suit and tie, while the younger lad wears baggy pants, bling, and earrings. They had played together a number of times with not much conversation, but eventually started talking and getting to know each other. They now arrange times to meet and play together and seem to enjoy each others company. I have seen this many times and just think it is cool.

Real World Blackjack: Here are a couple of points I didn't mention about my Real World Blackjack System. One is, I normally start out the new shoe by going back to betting my basic betting unit. Even if I ended a shoe at the seven unit level, I start the new shoe betting one unit.

Even though I normally follow my Basic Strategy, hand in and hand out, I do make exceptions occasionally. For instance, if I had been losing and then get on a good run where I am up to a high betting unit level and a double down opportunity occurs, sometimes I will just hit and not double. This is because I am finally above my winning limit goal and even if I lose the hand I will still be near my winning limit goal. If on the other hand, I would lose this large double, I would drop significantly back chip wise. Also, if my playing time limit is up and I am ready to leave, it makes sense to me to only hit and not double in this situation. Also, if I'm near the end of my playing time and I again have a fairly large bet that if won will get me to my winning goal, and I have a Blackjack and the Dealer is showing an Ace, I will take "even money" to assure myself of reaching my goal. Normally, I would never take "even money", but in this particular case, it is justified. So there may be times to vary your Basic Strategy a bit, but in the majority of time following my real world guidelines is advisable.

CHAPTER 7

Conclusion

I HOPE YOU have enjoyed this book and will have taken away some useful information. My goal was to help people play better winning Blackjack. I believe my Real World analysis and the strategies that came out of this analysis will help you win more and lose less. I encourage you to have the discipline and patience to put my suggestions to practice and see if they work for you. As I have stated before, there are no guarantees when you enter a Casino, but try my suggestions for twenty or thirty playing sessions, chart the results, and see if they don't help you play winning Blackjack. Maybe over a period of time you find a few tweaks to my program that seems to work for you. By all means, if you find something that consistently works for you, then use it. The goal is to win, and over the long term make a tidy profit.

Thank you for reading this book.

Made in the USA
Lexington, KY
01 November 2012